The Story of Flax Bourton

THE author was born in Dartford, Kent, and educated at the King's School, Rochester. After National Service, he trained at St Paul's College, Cheltenham, and began his teaching career at Bexleyheath Secondary School for Boys. The family moved to Flax Bourton in January 1959 when Brian took up a post at Backwell Secondary School; he subsequently taught there for over thirty years. He and his wife, Brenda, continue to live locally.

Although unknown to them at the time, it was fitting, given Brian's historical interests, that they should have taken up residence in 'Burh-ton', for it was Brian's great grandfather (thirty-three times removed) who improved and developed the Burghal Hidage, an Anglo-Saxon document dating from the reigns of King Alfred the Great and his son, Edward.

The Story

of

Flax Bourton

A Village and its People

Brian Mayled

Wind*flower*

First published in 2009 by

Windflower Books, The Rectory, Main Road, Flax Bourton, North Somerset BS48 3QJ

Copyright © Brian Mayled 2009

British Library Cataloguing in Publication Data

A catalogue record for this book is available from the British Library

ISBN 978–0–9560967–0–8

Printed and bound in Great Britain by

Burleigh Press, Portishead, North Somerset

Contents

꧂

Preface

❧

THIS little publication is an attempt to outline the local history of a small North Somerset village; it is, in truth, no more than an introduction to the story of a settlement and its people.

Every unit (family, house or road) of every community bears its own stories: some intriguing, others mundane; some worth recounting, others kept well within bounds. This is not the occasion for such writings. If, however, by reading this brief account of our village you feel inspired to take up the challenge and do your own research to add more details to the sketch, then this publication will be more than justified.

With each generation comes a host of characters, and a few from the past make an appearance in these pages from time to time. I have endeavoured to avoid mentioning by name any current members of the community, except those who have contributed towards this book. Also, it is important to note that I have kept the account within what is now called the civil parish boundary.

I am indebted to a number of present and past residents for their assistance with research and other help without which this enterprise would not have been possible: Maurice Atherton, Peter Clist, Ruth Hill, Bob Parker, Doug Reed, Joan Stevens and Peter Smith, who provided material and information; Richard Greatrex for guidance in publishing; Mary-Jane Greatrex for her advice, time and effort in editing the manuscript; and all those who have encouraged me to put down my thoughts on this subject in writing. The views expressed, I hasten to add, are entirely my own.

My interest in local history was sown by the most unlikely of people who proved to be a born teacher – a Mr Biss, Head Verger of Rochester Cathedral many years ago. In just one afternoon this remarkable man made the story of that building explode into life; I cannot speak for my fellow sixth-formers accompanying me on the tour, but I personally have been hooked ever since.

Brian Maylec
September 2008

Introduction

&

Starting Out

MUCH of our village as we know it today is not yet fifty years old; in fact, a good deal is under thirty years old. In that time, however, its land area has increased by a fifth, its population has doubled and the number of dwellings has gone up correspondingly. In addition, the environment has changed dramatically: gone are its orchards, vanished are its farms, dried up or hidden are its watercourses and ford. Even, sadly, place and property names have changed. Nevertheless, our natural curiosity must wonder what the village used to be, what it was like, when it all started.

My personal interest in the subject is long standing and spans nearly half a century, so when a number of villagers urged me to set my impromptu ramblings down in written form I was not averse to making a start. But what really made me delve deeper into Flax Bourton's history was my research for the current guide to St Michael's Church: the more I looked at the building, the more it seemed to elude previous historical descriptions. Thus began my quest in earnest, with the church at its centre.

In this, the resulting exploration, I have attempted to piece together fragments, traditions, miscellaneous facts and figures, suppositions and deductions from documentary sources or collective memory, which, I hope, will allow us to build up – albeit somewhat sketchily in places – a picture of Flax Bourton from its earliest times. The rich heritage which we will discover along the way can only serve to enhance our appreciation of what we already know to be a truly lovely pocket of the northern tip of Somerset.

This gate at the top of Combe Lane gave access to the wood and village quarry.

1

Roots

THE beginning of this story is one of mystery and detection, one whose roots took hold long ago and yet one in which you and I are now a part. This is the story of a people and their place, of home.

Time travel has always been a dream of humans but, so far, it has been limited to the science of archaeology which is often the only route we can use to find clues to the distant past. To understand those clues, we have to try to transport ourselves back to the context or period in question; and in our quest for a definitive beginning to our own village settlement, that seems to be a very long time ago indeed.

In order to survive, we must have food and water, so, for some 6,000 years, settlements have been established where both can be obtained. With the exception of coastal settlers, the main source of food has come from the land through agriculture, and that has always been reliant on two factors: climate and soil.

Since the end of the last Ice Age, the valleys of Somerset and throughout the British Isles have been filling up with soil washed off the hills and sediments brought in by the sea, a process that never stops. This is why archaeologists usually have to 'dig' for evidence; and the deeper one digs the farther back in time one goes.

So what of this valley of ours – the Yeo/Kenn Valley? We know that attempts to drain and reclaim the 'Levels' or marshes certainly took place during the Roman period because remains of a villa have been found by the Yeo near Congresbury. But sediments also show that during the last 2,000 years the sea has repeatedly swamped the valley, most famously in 1607 when a 35ft tsunami devastated the land. Indeed, right up to the early 1950s water regularly flooded the valley in winter.

When the Romans first saw this valley, it would have been a vast marsh of reed, alder and sallow with streams snaking through the vegetation. But the adjacent hills were not uninhabited: there was the large palisaded settlement of Cadbury above what is now Tickenham and lead was being extracted from the south-eastern hill range, evidence of which can still be seen in Bourton Combe Wood. In 350 years of occupation the Romans certainly contributed towards the silting up of the valley by constructing a sea wall.

2

Digging Deeper

THE vital question now follows: when was the settlement of Bourton originally established? Truthfully, we cannot be certain as to the precise answer; neither do we know why it began. Happily, though, we can take several illuminating clues emerging from our quest and see where they lead us.

Some years ago Mr Ray Spencer of Castle Farm consulted an archaeological diviner about a water source. Besides finding water, the expert also claimed to have discovered post-holes which he dated between AD 500 and AD 1000 – admittedly a rather generous period of time (the equivalent of, say, Henry VIII's reign to the present day) but the claim should not be dismissed.

The name 'Bourton' is the next clue. Scholars of place names suggest that the word is a corruption of Anglo-Saxon, an amalgam of 'burgh' and 'ton', meaning 'fortified farm' or 'fenced settlement'. The fence would probably have been on top of a bank created by digging a ditch and would now be described as a 'stockade'. Such structures were usually erected for defence purposes, which begs another question: why were they erected here?

Bourton is situated at the head of the valley farthest away from attack via the sea, assuming the existence of other settlements along the hillsides as long established as ours. Of course, just over the hill to the east north-east was Wansdyke which may have acted as a boundary between the kingdoms of Mercia and Wessex. If it did, that could certainly have presented real or potential danger. It might also be the case that Bourton served as the residence of a thane (a local Saxon administrator, a kind of Lord of the Manor) but, if there were ever any written record, it no longer exists. So, at the present time, there is no unequivocal reason why Bourton should have been fortified.

One piece of evidence that has not yet been brought into the frame, however, and the only witness that has survived at the heart of the village for a millennium, is the one truly ancient building: the Church of St Michael and All Angels. Let us see if this can reveal any further clues to Bourton's distant origins.

Up to AD 1000 almost all buildings in 'Engla-lond' were constructed from wood or wood and daub, but soon afterwards an architectural revolution took place: ecclesiastical buildings started to be reconstructed using stone, often in the continental Romanesque style. Most were fairly small, narrow and high, with doorways to match.

St Michael's certainly has the features mentioned, recognizable when the north aisle is ignored. The doorway, although somewhat restored, is clearly a classic Saxon structure, while the sculpture of St Michael above it on the porch side has been dated to the late Saxon period (i.e. mid-eleventh century). Approached from the outside, the doorway appears to be Norman; but a more careful inspection indicates that the façade has been 'stuck on' and, in fact, does not accurately fit the inner structure.

Dr Kate Tiller, in her book *English Local History*, records that from *c.* 1025 private local churches were frequently established as expressions of seigniorial status. It should also be noted that within twenty years of 1066, William I had replaced the English aristocracy with Norman Barons.

Within these considerations, then, may lie another clue. Is the superimposed Norman façade a rushed job to emphasize Norman authority? Could Bourton have been a thane's dwelling and this indeed a reason for fortification? There is no entry for Bourton in the Domesday Book but at the end of the record for Wraxall this note appears:

> To this manor has been added 1 hide which a thane held before 1066. Land for 1 plough. Value 10s.

(In Somerset a hide was an area of land of 40 to 60 acres – enough for one fairly large household.) Unfortunately, over the thousand years since then any further records, if they ever existed, have vanished. William I deliberately had many

Saxon documents destroyed and what survived his purge Henry VIII attempted to trash with a high degree of success. Interestingly, William was particularly harsh on the West Country because of an uprising in 1068 against his 'usurping the throne of England'. Nevertheless, this first record indicates that Bourton could well have been a sub-manor of Wraxall, which in reality meant it was a settlement of labourers who owed fealty to the Lord of the Manor, the Bishop of Coutances.

What we can conclude with confidence, then, is that there has definitely been a settlement on the site since at least the first millennium AD and possibly considerably longer. Some of the lead-mining activity up on the hill to the south is probably Celtic, while Neolithic flints found washed down into the valley indicate even earlier activity.

St Michael's Church boasts a number of Saxon stone carvings, including this one, clearly depicting the head of a fox.

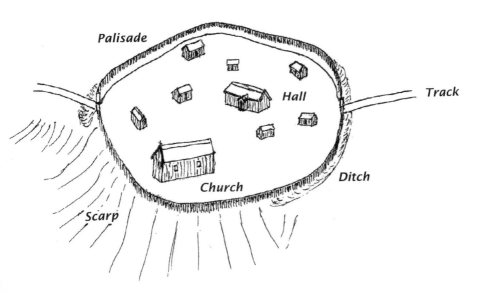

A rough impression of Saxon Bourton. Anglo-Saxon settlements usually included workshops, living accommodation and store houses, all in separate buildings. The population was often very small — only two, three or a few more families.

A typical Saxon building of wood or wattle and daub and thatched. Buildings were rectangular and usually of only one room. Living houses had a hearth for cooking, heating and lighting while larger or more important settlements had a hall.

The inner doorway of St Michael's Church displays the marks of a classic Saxon structure.

The magnificent Saxon sculpture of St Michael overcoming the devil in the form of a dragon.

3

❧

Surveying the Ancient Landscape

THE most ancient part of the village perches on top of what was once an irregular foothill scarp under Broadfield Down, effectively sandwiched between the upper and lower spring lines. The promontory that extends to the south, west and north of the settlement is covered with Keuper Marl which forms a reddish, fertile soil.

In AD 1000 it is probable that about 40 acres of land were actually cultivated, most likely to the west of the settlement. Livestock would have grazed the hillside to the south; some woodland clothed the steeper slopes. Lead-mining had cleared much of the tree cover on the top of the hill but the combe supported a nuclear yew population, while Pigsfoot Wood clung on with its remnant of small-leaved lime to the 'Wild Wood' of prehistory. Whether Combe Lane and Park Lane were once estate boundary ditches is difficult to say without an archaeological dig.

As the population grew so more land was brought under the plough to both west and east of the village; indeed, some ridge and furrow is preserved under the secondary woodland growth of Breach Hill. However, of the 590 acres of the parish, as it finally became (until the boundary changes of 1980), only part was actually cultivated. Some was wooded, some marsh and at least 11 per cent was common grazing land. Not until the Enclosures Acts and nineteenth-century demands did the landscape change yet again.

Before extensive modern quarrying and climate change at least three springs flowed up on the hill. One still intermittently issues from the upper reaches of the combe and is called the 'Stancombe', a name which refers to its stony course. In 1968 it gouged out a new channel at the bottom of the gorge, still visible today. Revd J. Collinson, writing in 1791, described the Stancombe as flowing into the 'Nailsea Water' (the Barrow Brook): it would almost certainly have followed the main road to Post Office Lane, continuing to run – according to the 1885 map – between Church Farm and Charlton Cottage, proceeding north-eastwards to Rock Cottage and finally heading due north to the river.

The second spring rises on the slope below Barrow Court above Breach Hill Wood, flows down to Wayside Cottage, progresses beside Station Road through the new school grounds and, originally, into the Barrow Brook. This spring rarely ceases to flow.

Nowadays both streams are culverted for much of their courses through the village and most people have no idea that they exist. When Brunel cut his railway through to Exeter he solved the problem of severing the streams (a third runs down from beside Westbrook) by channelling them all into a giant drain.

Originally the settlement was linked to neighbouring habitations by a track that followed the drier foothills. Over time the track assumed a more important status, being the most direct link that avoided marshland between the villages on the south side of the valley. Eventually it became a 'Post Road' with mail coaches thundering along to and from Bristol. Now much of it is the A370, a 'red' major road.

Looking eastward along the main road towards the church, during the punishing winter of 1963.

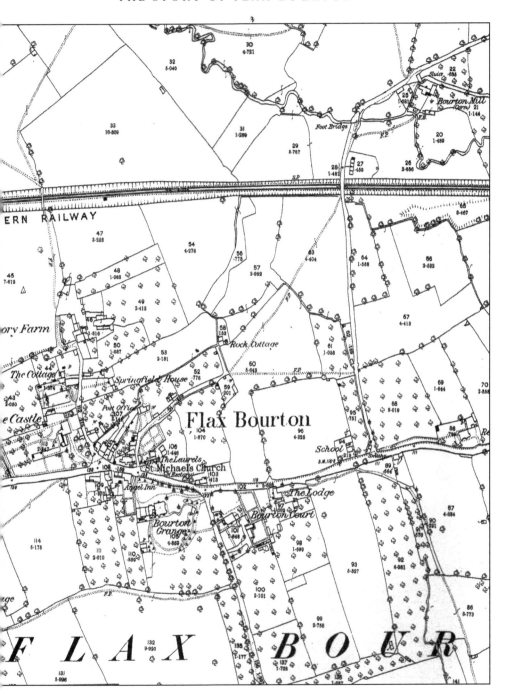

1885 Ordnance Survey map. Note the footbridge to the east of the ford, the smithy the numerous orchards. 'P' indicates a pump.

4

Coming of Age

THE Middle Ages could be expected to offer a more detailed picture of village life. Again, however, informed guesswork has the upper hand since documentary material continues to elude even the most determined of researchers. Written records are almost as sparse for this period as for pre-mediaeval times – possibly owing to a demotion in status of the settlement – and of the few that do exist only one is of any real significance.

Edward III's Exchequer Lay Subsidies of 1327–8 were well recorded. They comprised a tax of one-twentieth of all movable property on those whose goods were worth 10s. or more. The list for Bourton names sixteen men who were charged between 6d. and 6s. 8d. This is not surprising: a booming economy during the twelfth and thirteenth centuries had brought a population explosion and by 1300 it was around four million in England (four times the figure for AD 1000).

A succession of bad harvests during the early part of the fourteenth century in many areas of the country resulted in the Great Famine of 1315–16. It turned out to be a portent of things to come: Bristol was the first large town in England to experience the Black Death. That was in 1348 and within a year at least half the city's population was dead. It is inconceivable that nearby villages were not affected; indeed, St Michael's fabric gives an indication as to Bourton's fate.

Over the whole of England there was disquiet among survivors and the Church was blamed for not preventing the Plague. Some communities had been wiped out while others were grossly reduced. Since rural settlements were small anyway, often there were barely enough people left to grow food. Ecclesiastical buildings were neglected as communities struggled to survive. The Black Death of 1348 was followed by further outbreaks at twenty- to twenty-five-year intervals.

Nevertheless, the people of Bourton recovered sufficiently to support the parish priest in restoring the neglected church fabric. In those days both priest and people were responsible for the maintenance and repair of their church building. Between 1350 and 1450 they set to, restoring the dilapidated structure in the architectural style of the day and, at the same time, adding a tower to the west end of the Saxon building. So the church acquired new windows and the great perpendicular arch at the west end of the nave. Apart from this, they carried out necessary repairs to make the church usable again, constructing a new roof and ceiling in the process. All this became clear in the stonework when the church was repointed during the autumn of 2006.

Since the village had its own quarry there is a possibility that Castle Farm, Church Farm and Priory Farm also contain some stonework from this period but, in the main, domestic building continued for another 150 years to be timber-framed with wattle and daub infill.

Mention of Priory Farm throws a puzzling etymological question into the spotlight. As we have noted, the origin of the name 'Bourton' derives from the Anglo-Saxon for 'fortified farm' or 'fenced settlement'. The 'Flax' prefix, however, is obscure since no evidence can be traced to establish the existence of a linen industry here, as the name would seem to imply. This is where Priory Farm comes in: Revd Collinson in his *History and Antiquities of the County of Somerset,* published in 1791, recounts the Abbey of Flaxley in Gloucestershire exchanging land at Regil (Winford) for around 100 acres of farmland (i.e. Priory Farm) in Bourton, the latter thereby indicating its connection with the abbey by retaining the prefix 'Flax'. What the monks would have been like as landlords is anybody's guess since many monasteries by the end of the fourteenth century had become morally lax, to say the least: a visitation of Flaxley Abbey in 1397 revealed that nine monks were 'fornicators' and the Abbot was 'defamatus' with three different women!

Be that as it may, this compelling hypothesis has to remain just that; Collinson's source is unknown and he makes no reference to a date. Moreover, a history of the Abbey written a century later offers no mention of any exchange. The origin of our village's full name, then, continues as another intriguing quasi-mystery.

5

☙

Domestic Developments

T HE comparative stability of the Tudor years, coupled
with a mini-'ice age', brought about a veritable building
revolution with regard to domestic dwellings. Both the Angel
Inn, opposite the church, and Church Farm exhibit features
from that time. Gladly, it is from the Tudor period onwards
that historical records of note begin to survive.

In 1532 'a bushel of whete' was bequeathed to the
'chappell of Burtown' while in 1533 a 'William Jenyngs of
Burton' gave to 'his ghostly father Sir William Webster
[Chaplain of Bourton] four pence and two drays of wood'.
There also appear records of small land bequests among
members of certain individual families connected with the
village. Chronologically, there was a family named Tynte,
related to a Wraxall freeholder (a franklin), then a family
named Cox, and finally a family named Sparrow. The latter
held the Bourton estate for quite some time.

The village community continued its daily self-sufficient
labouring existence and by the end of the seventeenth
century probably boasted some thirteen dwellings, mostly
clustered about the church. Castle Farm, Priory Farm,

The Laurels, Grove Cottage and possibly Porch Cottage (the forge shop) date at least from the seventeenth to early eighteenth centuries; in addition, there may well have been some building on the site of Bourton Court (now Bourton House) during the century.

The eighteenth century saw more building. The Sparrow family, having acquired the estate, wanted a dwelling in the village, so a fine new house was commissioned to be located on the west side of what became Post Office Lane. With grounds bounded by a high wall, it was named The Castle – a rather bland stone cube of a building, but containing some woodcarving by Grinling Gibbons.

Around the late 1700s and early 1800s a notable phase of domestic construction began since by that time the village population was closely approaching 200. Most dwellings were built near the church where there was dry ground, with one or two outliers to the east. Eastfield and Westbrook are described as being 'a short distance from the village upon the road to Bristol'; both are nineteenth-century enlargements of unpretentious cottages. Between these and the village, at the junction with White's Lane (now Station Road), was one of two village smithies, ideally located for road traffic. When this industry finally dwindled, the building became a private dwelling called Primrose Cottage; it is now the Old School House – a misnomer, in fact, seeing as the building has never been used for educational purposes at all.

Such name changes are far from scarce and it is an interesting diversion to note how some have evolved. To take several examples: Bourton House is shown on early maps as Bourton Court, not that it was ever used as such. It was probably named 'Court' by its owners, the Gores of Barrow Court, who would take up residence each winter because the Barrow property was too cold. Adjacent to it is Flaxley Cottage, now Flax Lea. Then there are two properties in Post Office Lane: the present St Michael's House was originally simply The Cottage while Rose Cottage was built as Springfield House because it was hard by a field with a spring. Such instances only go to show that property names can during the course of time fall prey to numerous influences, not necessarily retaining any connection with the original function or nature of a building.

Returning to our picture of the Tudor village, one property that had to stand on marshland was the grist mill because it harnessed the water power of the Barrow Brook. The earliest date I can find for a mill at Bourton is 1327, implying that it already existed. The last actual mill building was a three-storey structure, sadly long since demolished.

Rock Cottage presents a curious puzzle: who might have lived there? Set in such a wet location surrounded by springs and watercourses when built, it was an isolated property to be sure. On the tithe map it is marked as being held by Hodges of the road junction smithy which, incidentally, was well placed because it had a permanent supply of water from the spring above Breach Hill Wood.

Despite the accelerated growth of pre-industrial England, it is chastening to reflect that our village remained largely self-sufficient as it had been throughout its long existence, right back to the first millennium. Besides the farms which produced its food, there was a carpenter's shop (Grange Farm), two black-smiths, a brewery (The Laurels), a slaughter house (Church Farm), a tannery (St Michael's House) and the village quarry for building stone. The majority of households were able to make their own clothes; footwear was locally sourced; meat (Hereford House was the butcher, its front garden brimming with butcher's broom) and groceries were locally produced, much of the latter by each household. Entertainment was homemade too, as it always had been in rural communities. People lived in, with and understood their environment. Good, workable, fertile land was used for arable crops. There were 67 acres of common land for grazing, fifteen well-stocked, extensive orchards, and Bourton Hill Plantation was cropped by coppicing in compartment rotation for timber (building material and furniture), wood (for fencing, tools, wattle and fuel) and charcoal. Besides the plantation there was Breach Hill secondary woodland and a large copse to the east of the mill. Even the really ancient Pigsfoot Wood was managed.

Roads were unmade and in places the cart and carriage traffic wore the surface down to bedrock, which on the hill is not far down.

For centuries the water supply came from wells. Some places were lucky enough to have their own while others used the village well, which acquired a pump in the nineteenth century and lasted into the twentieth. Not all sources were uncontaminated: there are records of payment for prayers to ward off 'the cholera'. In the 1800s there were nineteen wells, thirteen of which were capped by a pump by 1885.

To reach the mill the Barrow Brook had to be forded, and eventually a footbridge was constructed across the river to the east of the present bridge. At the end of the nineteenth century a road bridge was put across the ford, the footbridge removed and a new ford made in its place. This is now mostly overgrown and partially blocked by a fence that has crept out from the adjacent holding. Fords were not only water crossings but served as invaluable spots for washing wagons and wagon-wheels.

Hereford House and the Old Post Office were both built around the turn of the eighteenth century, but the three properties of Church Walk were added in the early nineteenth, as was Charlton Cottage. Milestone Cottage (Six Mile Cottage) was an eighteenth-century structure and served as the original poorhouse before the erection of a terrace of four two-roomed cottages down near the river bridge in 1821. Opposite the earlier cottage is the milestone marking 6 miles to Bristol. The stone is listed, as are comparable surviving stones like the one in Backwell.

Between the Angel Inn and Castle Farm there was a shop which is shown on the 1885 map. At some point in the late 1800s, it was taken over by a Mr Moody who had moved out from Bristol. He ran a high-class grocery establishment until it was demolished in the early twentieth century when he moved the business into a coffin-maker's workshop in Church Lane, next to Grove Cottage where the family were living at that period.

Donald Moody's high-class grocer shop in Church Lane with Grove Cottage on the left. Notice that Church Lane was not made up when this photograph was taken in 1960.

The end of Church Lane in 1959. The cottage appears on the 1838 tithe map and was occupied in 1959 by Mr and Mrs Rice; Mr Rice worked on Priory Farm with Mr Maurice Atherton. Rock Cottage is off frame to the right. Bourton Mead now stands where the photographer was positioned.

The terrace of 'poorhouses' near the river bridge, now Bridge Cottages.

The central village pump opposite Hereford House (the butcher's shop) with the original Charlton Cottage to the left and Church Farm with the Post Office sign on the wall, c. 1900.

A fine view of the Old Post Office, c. 1922. The windows, gables and roof pitch suggest a sixteenth-century origin.

6

𝕏

Brunel Comes to Bourton

No story of Flax Bourton would be at all satisfactory without some mention of its railway and the impact it had on the village.

The early part of the nineteenth century saw the birth of a form of transport which, unrealized at the time, boldly announced the arrival of the 'modern age'. In just thirty years the speed of public transport increased fourfold thanks to the steam engine. The successful development and expansion of the Great Western Railway Company (GWR) in the mid-1830s brought about the formation of the Bristol and Exeter Railway Company soon after. I.K. Brunel was employed as the engineer and the route opened in 1841 with broad gauge track. It transformed this parish. A huge trench was blasted and dug from east to west across the lower part of the land, thus severing the northern area of the parish from the southern part and necessitating the construction of three linking bridges, as well as the diversion of the watercourses already mentioned. The project, carried out by Irish navvies, must have caused horrendous disruption to village life while the work took place; no wonder prayers were requested again for protection from cholera, a disease notoriously associated with navvies and not at that time known to be water-borne.

Flax Bourton's first railway station was, in fact, a couple of hundred yards nearer Cambridge Batch tunnel and rightly speaking in Long Ashton parish. It was opened in 1860 but moved to its present site in 1893, a location allowing more space for a siding and coal yard. By that date most domestic heating was from coal-burning.

The Bristol and Exeter was absorbed by the GWR in 1876, a year after the track had become mixed gauge. Although diesel traction began to appear now and again in the late 1950s, most trains continued to be steam-hauled. Top-link drivers reckoned on climbing the Cambridge Batch incline from Temple Meads fast enough to reach 70mph by the time they passed Backwell on the downhill run. Regrettably, standards of maintenance had declined by 1959 and a characteristic clanking noise issued forth from some of the locomotives when travelling at speed. Nevertheless, in an age of far fewer cars, an operative village station was a huge asset; these days, with too many cars, it would indeed be once again.

The MoD oil tanks and sidings materialized at the time of the Suez Crisis but since then have seen little activity. However, Brunel's road bridge is no longer: hit by a derailed freight train in 1974, the damage was so extensive that replacement was the only answer.

The twentieth century witnessed one other significant intrusion into the village's agricultural idyll, well before the commuter invasion destroyed rural bliss for good. A certain Robert Hobbs acquired the land to the west of the combe and began aggregate extraction. For over half a century now the community has been regularly shaken by explosions which have progressively removed parts of the hill massive. Over time, lorries have become larger and more frequent so that Main Road properties are increasingly vibrated to their very foundations.

view looking east to the station yard with a down express in the early part of the entieth century. Note the horse and cart 'goods' service!

7

In the Classroom

FROM the time of St Augustine's arrival in England in AD 597 school education was carried out by priests, especially those in monasteries since, for the most part, they were the only places equipped with any sort of academia. The majority of the population were illiterate; in fact, few kings prior to Henry II could read or write. By the thirteenth century, however, schools for boys were emerging from a variety of foundations and Oxford and Cambridge Universities were established. Nevertheless, for the next 700 years only very few children were lucky enough to receive a school education.

In 1851 Mrs Smyth of Ashton Court offered a site for a school opposite the present cricket field. Unfortunately, nothing came of her generosity, but in 1858 another site was donated by Sir John Greville Smyth. As a result, what we now know as the 'Old School' was finally built in 1859 using donations amounting to £346 8s. 7d. The Church of England was the main contributor. The 'New Room' (30ft x 15ft) was designed to accommodate sixty children but soon proved inadequate for such numbers. It is noteworthy that in those early years many of the school's pupils came from neighbouring villages.

At first children could attend the school from the age of three and generally stayed until they were ten, when they were expected to begin work. The first Education Act of 1870 was vague on matters of attendance and leaving age, but in 1880 primary education was made compulsory; shortly after that in 1891 pupils were exempted from all expense entailed in their tutoring. Despite the Act, however, a whole array of seasonal diversions tended to affect attendance in a rural school, which could be disrupted by haymaking, fruit-picking, rabbit-shooting and other farming activities.

School life, though, was not the proverbial bed of roses. If you survived infancy all kinds of hazards lay in waiting, especially illnesses. Year after year there were periodic epidemics which could and did result in the Medical Officer of Health closing the school: 'Brain Fever' (one assumes Meningitis or Encephalitis), Measles, Mumps, Whooping Cough, Scarlet Fever, Diphtheria, French Influenza, Ringworm and 'bad feet' are all recorded as occurring repeatedly. Apparently, 'acute sickness' also often broke out. Rickets was not uncommon until the issue of milk, from 1934 onwards, remedied the vitamin D deficiency in some children's diets.

Although a mains water supply was laid along Bourton's major road at the end of the nineteenth century, the school was not connected until 1925.

During the Second World War as many as thirty-eight evacuees are recorded as attending the school. Shortly after that, in 1947, the school ceased to be all-age and became a Voluntary Controlled Infants School. Financial support was withdrawn from the Board of Managers and became the responsibility of Somerset Education Committee. At the beginning of the 1960s the status changed again to become primary for five- to eleven-year-olds. (At that time the secondary leaving age was fifteen, the student being free to leave at the end of the term in which he or she reached the statutory age.)

The present school site began life in 1973 as a playing field on which there was one temporary classroom; the split-site arrangement continued over the next twenty years.

The Victorian building which housed the school for more than a century, now a private house. This photograph was taken in 1959.

8

❧

Village Gossip

HALF a century ago houses still clustered around the church, just as they had done for over a thousand years. There was some ribbon development eastward along Main Road and beside Station Road, with a few other dwellings scattered around the parish, including a reading room (now Doubledoor Cottage), such literary institutes being popular in the early part of the twentieth century.

There were several orchards in the village. One, of cider apples, stretched from the east side of Grange Farm north to Church Lane; it was not unknown for crows to get drunk on the 'drops' beneath those trees! Bourton proved no exception to the ancient Somerset custom of wassailing. On old twelfth night (17 January), cider would be poured on to the roots of the finest orchard tree and spiced wassail cake placed in the branches to encourage a good apple crop. Then a great noise was raised to frighten away any lurking evil spirits, while the chant

Hats full, caps full, three bushel bags full!

was sung in unison by all the onlookers.

Opposite the church was the Angel Inn boasting an Elizabethan fireplace and serving Williams' cider. Hartley Williams made his cider on Backwell Common from his own orchards and many others around the area. When I first came to the village in 1959, it was customary for congregation and priest alike to adjourn across the road to the Angel for a taste of the local brew after Evensong every Sunday – a tradition sorely missed!

With five working farms, the community still had a strong agricultural link and everyone knew each other. Characters abounded. Living down in one of the poorhouses was a formidable lady, Emily Derrick, a short, rather portly figure who acted as verger at the church and guarded her office rigorously. She was never without a hat that closely resembled a tea-cosy and she smoked like a chimney, though not during a service I hasten to add. She would feed the rats that inhabited the vacant poorhouses at the same time as feeding her cats. Needless to say, the rats flourished and grew to a gigantic size. When Emily died in 1972 she was buried in a family grave in the churchyard, the last person to be afforded that privilege.

Beside Stancombe Lane, in a rather Spartan old Nissen hut, lived an idiosyncratic couple of some mystery. Arthur (always referred to as Art) and Mrs Bennett kept what might be termed as something of a smallholding. Art was never to be seen in the village without a wheelbarrow which, because of his rather dwarf-like stature and appearance, always looked far too big for him. He 'did' the gardens of a number of villagers who aspired to a more elevated social status. All agreed that he grew superb tomatoes, though the source of his fertilizer was never closely questioned.

Immediately opposite Stancombe Lane lies the village cricket field where many a battle has been fought. During the interwar years, the dominant force in the Cricket Club was the Robinson family. To mark the close association of the family with the club, an annual match would be contested between the Robinsons and the village. Esmond, the head of the clan, was an accomplished batsman at his peak, while the club boasted a young fast bowler, Joe Lansberry (who later married Hephsibah Patch, the daughter of the licensee of the Ich Dien in Barrow Gurney). In one of these annual matches, Esmond was sweetly stroking the ball to all corners of the ground and heading for a century when Joe was brought on and began steaming in, determined to stop Esmond getting his ton. The village captain drew Joe aside to temper the young bowler's killer instinct: 'Go easy, lad,' he advised, 'If you let him get the ton it'll be drinks all round. Once he gets there, then you can shatter his stumps!' During the Second World War many clubs were, in effect, suspended, but after 1945 Flax Bourton CC quickly regained its status as one of the leading village clubs. Sadly, since the 1980s the club's fortunes have fluctuated, but more recent reorganization has steadied the boat and on-site cricket continues in the twenty-first century.

Apart from cricket, there were other, equally absorbing Sunday 'entertainments' for local folk. Jack Walker and his wife, of Grange Farm, spawned a world champion plough-man, worked the farm very much as a partnership, and had a vocabulary to rival any trooper. They owned about ten milking cows and one of their pasture fields lay adjacent to the cricket pitch. It sometimes happened that the cattle would be grazing in that same field on a tranquil summer Sunday afternoon when, come milking time, Jack would push his bike up the road to collect the cows, conversing with his wife in very ripe language at the top of his voice. On a given signal Mrs Walker would swing the farmyard gate across the main road to stop all traffic travelling towards Backwell, while Jack directed his cows down the main road. Of course, no self-respecting cow, heavy with milk, is going to hurry, and hedgerow plants are always worth investigating, so progress tended to be sedate at the best of times. During the 1960s family car transport was increasing, so a sunny Sunday afternoon attracted many Bristolians to Weston. As the traffic backed up behind the lumbering herd, Jack's exchanges with hot, exasperated drivers afforded plenty of comic relief for a gathering audience, matched only by his wife's heated dealings with those detained behind the gate. Happy days! Jack was actually a mine of information on country-lore. Most significantly, it was he who, having fields by the combe, used yew posts for fencing in preference to oak, maintaining that yew heartwood long outlasted oak.

Castle Farm was worked by the three Winstone siblings (two brothers and their sister). When I encountered them in the 1960s they were 'getting on a bit' and had not changed their habits since childhood. In wet weather, for instance, they would cover head and shoulders with a hessian sack, as country people had done for centuries, and I never saw one of them sporting a raincoat.

Besides the Angel Inn the village still had several community 'hot spots'. The Post Office was a vital asset: by 1959, it was situated next to Hereford House, having previously been in the west end of Church Farm – hence the door against the road. There was also, of course, Moody's the 'Grocer of quality' offering all manner of provisions. Almost outside the village, literally on the parish boundary, was another inn, the Jubilee, which provided road traffic parking and snacks.

The Grange had ceased to be a private dwelling and had become the offices of Long Ashton Rural District Council. Somerset extended up to the Bristol City boundary, the designation of Avon being still very much in the future. The Grange, built in 1866, replaced an earlier, smaller dwelling occupied by the bailiff of the Wraxall estate.

Although fifty years ago Main Road and Post Office Lane were metalled and surfaced with Tarmacadam, Church Lane remained unmade for several more years.

Up to the 1950s Grove Cottage had been a terrace of three cottages and until Holly House was built for the Moody family they lived in the first of the three. When the three cottages were sold to the Miller family, there was still a tenant in one of them. Dr Keith Miller, one of the local GPs with a young family, set about making some internal alterations, especially as certain floor-timbers needed replacement. A local firm was employed and one of the workmen was given the job of removing the rotting bedroom floor. Wielding a saw with novice enthusiasm, he proceeded to cut all around the affected part but, sure enough, had positioned himself in the middle of the marked area. The inevitable happened and he, with the floor, descended rapidly to the flagstones 7ft below. By chance, the doctor was not far away but the youth appeared to be none the worse for the experience; gladly, medical assistance was surplus to requirements on that occasion.

Porch Cottage was originally a forge shop. The building beside it still shows a drainage gully in part of the floor and a furnace alcove at the back. The blacksmith served the needs of the village surrounding the forge. When the shop closed, the building became two cottages, one of two rooms and the other of three; at the beginning of the twentieth century a fourth room was added to the second cottage. When we purchased them in 1959, they had been linked into one by inserting a connecting door on each floor, but both staircases were still *in situ* and remained so for another thirty-five years.

Our first few months at Porch Cottage were none too comfortable: the winter weather was cold and frosty and living conditions somewhat primitive compared with present-day standards. There was a cold tap in the kitchen, no bathroom, no inside lavatory, no flush, no hot-water system, and just a small solid-fuel heater in the kitchen. But we did have the luxury of electricity. Even in 1959 these conditions were not unusual for rural labourers' dwellings.

When we did upgrade the property subsequently we discovered a 400-year-old drain from Castle Farm running under the corner of the old shop. Because the kitchen was unevenly flagged a cement screed had been put over it – a not uncommon feature for properties of considerable age. On removing the floor a few years ago, a 'cobbled' bone floor was revealed underneath, made mainly of cattle bone sunk on end and side by side. The flagstones had simply been laid on top.

Porch Cottages were an example of the kind of labourers' dwellings that typified most of the village accommodation from the seventeenth century. One room down, one room up, an earth closet and an open fireplace. Nothing else!

The mediaeval cottage that was formerly the Angel Inn.

Primrose Cottage is the old smithy on the right; School House is the nearest part of the black and white timbered building beyond the school.

Local cider was sourced from one of the many orchards that characterized the village. This one was located to the east of Grange Farm and stretched north to Church Lane.

Porch Cottage in 1962. The lovely flowering rose, Guinée, was only in its fourth year.

41

9

Culture Shock

THE decade of the 1960s is often held accountable for accelerating manifold changes in the way we live our lives today. For Bourton it was an especially significant time, setting in motion the wheels of rapid modernization and development – both literally and metaphorically.

The opening and early years of the decade were notable meteorologically. The winters of 1962 and 1963 were unusually severe for this customarily mild valley; 1963 was the worst winter since 1947 with six weeks of continuous frost and three separate heavy snowfalls. Drifts were so frozen that children could walk over five-barred gates as if crossing a bridge. Most of the spring seasons were wetter than usual. In July 1968 a storm dropped so much rain so quickly there was a flash flood: the River Chew washed away many of its bridges and here the Stancombe gouged out the bottom of the combe. Backwell Common was flooded to a depth of a metre and took days to drain away.

But, at the beginning of the decade, little did we know how much the village was to change. At the stroke of a pen the sale of the fields between Church Lane and Station Road brought about an irrevocable alteration to the village, the like of which it had not seen for at least 400 years. That signature seemed to mark the onset of a process in which the population doubled in half a decade, the culture of the once self-contained agricultural community vanished for ever, virtually overnight, and commuting suburbia took its place.

Admittedly, there had already been a small amount of development, with council and police houses on the east side of Station Road, but the inhabitants worked locally. The Meads (the development between Church Lane and Station Road) set a precedent. Since the mid-1960s, then, three developments off Post Office Lane, one off Church Lane, plus The Meads, Farleigh Hospital and some infill, have trebled the parish population. It cannot be disputed, in my view, that the character of the village has changed from one in tune with its natural environment to a semi-rural suburban satellite of nearby Bristol.

For centuries, the eastern boundary of the parish ran north from a point in a field near Barrow Court, down through Breach Hill Wood, across the field opposite the Jubilee Inn, along the side of its car park, and over the railway to the Barrow Brook Bridge on the Clevedon Road. This meant that up to 1980 the one-time Bedminster Workhouse (Long Ashton Public Assistance Institution, latterly Farleigh Hospital) had been in the civil parish of Long Ashton. With the revision of civil boundaries in 1980 the

43

eastern limit of Flax Bourton was moved to part of Barrow Court Lane, Barrow Lane, the edge of Cambridge Batch and along the railway cutting, before continuing to Clevedon Road.

So it was that Farleigh Hospital suddenly crossed boundaries. It had always been something of an autonomous settlement, however, and when it was closed and redeveloped so intensively and compactly, it almost inevitably retained its separate character.

The former Farleigh Hospital, now lying at the heart of Farleigh Green housing estate on the edge of the village.

10

> ❧

Tales of Mystery and Magic

A GENERAL upsurge of interest in the 'mystic' in recent times has given rise to a number of stories, theories and musings associated with our village. Brian Wright's book *Somerset Dragons* (2002) not surprisingly includes a couple of pages on Flax Bourton. The most obvious object of reference is St Michael's dragon in the church porch, which Wright describes admirably, having previously explained that in this case the dragon represents the devil.

Dragons, it seems, can occur in several guises: those with two legs are called Wyverns, a name derived from the Anglo-Saxon 'wivre' (a serpent) while legless dragons are known as 'worms' or 'flying serpents'. In this connection Wright draws attention to the carvings on the capitals of the chancel arch. The real significance of the occurrence inside the church is not indicated.

Phil Quinn's *Holy Wells of the Bath and Bristol Region* (1999) does make claims to establish the existence of holy wells in the village, but it must be said that his definition of a 'holy well' is incredibly loose. On the eastern margin of the parish, beside Westbrook, is a field called the Snakewell.

Quinn places a 'Snake well' spring behind Eastfield and suggests that its name might be associated with St Michael's dragon, although he refers to it as a serpent. He may be correct in his assertion but it is unlikely in my view, mainly because the Saxon sculpture was created centuries before cultivation extended eastward. Moreover, a thousand years ago the Snakewell area was wet and marshy: several rises are shown on maps as late as the end of the nineteenth century. Frogs frequent wet areas and grass snakes (our largest snake), eat frogs. It is reasonable to assume, then, that snakes could often be found in that location – hence the name.

Interestingly, there is another spring associated with the spirit world, though hardly a holy one. Until quite recently children were taken to the Stancombe Spring to see the fairies that were said to reside there. Although the periodic stream flows through the parish, the spring is actually just inside the Backwell boundary.

Another local Somerset lore has it that 'Chime Children' are those born between midnight on a Friday and cock-crow on a Saturday. Not only are they reputed to be able to see spirits, but they can also talk to fairies without being harmed. In addition, they are immune to ill-wishing, can wield power over animals and are gifted with knowledge of herbal lore and healing crafts.

The really spooky spectre of the village is well known to be a white horse which has been seen or heard clopping along the main road past the Angel Inn. Sceptics have suggested that a pint of scrumpy may have acquiesced in past sightings, but what of those who have merely heard the beast?

The most famous mystery of Bourton must surely be that of the 'Maid of the Haystack' – a young, very good-looking woman of 'refined manners' who lived under an old haystack for four years before being admitted to an asylum at Bitton. Hannah More became involved with her case and had her transferred to an institution in London, where the Maid died in 1800.

Several versions of the story have been published by authors not only from Bristol but as far afield as Belfast, London and even France. They all claim she was called Louisa and all agree she spent four years in a haystack in Flax Bourton. One account even states emphatically that she arrived in the village in 1776.

The heart of the mystery concerns the Maid's true identity: who was she and where did she really come from? The Bristol version of the tale asserts that she was an illegitimate daughter of Joseph I of Austria; the London/French account, a child of Emperor Francis I of Austria; and the *Belfast News*, the natural daughter of the Emperor of Germany. The French story is supposed to be dated 1785, while the earliest English one – by a Revd G.H. Glasse, Rector of Hanwell, Ealing – is dated 1801.

Although all accounts have a similar gist, the numerous embellishments vary, often dramatically. According to Revd Glasse, Louisa was demented when she arrived in Flax Bourton, but the *Belfast News* blames her four-year sojourn in the haystack for her dementia. The date also disagrees by some fifteen years.

Such variants aptly illustrate how legends can evolve, being woven together from diverse and sometimes conflicting sources. Fathoming the precise nature of the Maid's surreal settlement in Flax Bourton, along with her origins and demise, may well keep scholars and historians occupied for many years to come. Certainly, there is something haunting and compelling about her tale which continues to capture the popular imagination today.

A reproduction of William Palmer's 1788 engraving of Louisa, the unfortunate Maid of the Haystack. The image predates the first English written account by some thirteen years.

These chancel arch capitals in St Michael's Church show carvings of legless dragons known as 'worms' or 'flying serpents'.

11

Jewels in the Crown: Bourton Combe

BOURTON has two jewels in its crown: the combe and the church. The more ancient of the two, the combe, embraces flora, fauna and minerals of note. Probably formed by several ice ages, humans have exploited it for millennia. Some 8,000 years ago it was covered with the Wild Wood in which brown bear, wolf, auroch, red deer and wild boar all roamed. When *Homo sapiens* arrived the trees began to disappear and, eventually, so did the five mammal species just mentioned.

By the time the Celts discovered lead seams in the limestone, a good deal of the woodland on the top of the hill had been cleared. Today the remains of the lead industry can be seen in the present woodland as indentations, often with trees growing in the sediment and leaf-mould that has partially filled the excavations. Although there was one mine operating in the first part of the nineteenth century, all other activity had long ceased and secondary woodland had recolonized the area. In fact, reafforestation had been actively encouraged because of the economic importance of timber and wood for the reasons already stated. The 1838 tithe map shows Bourton Hill Plantation separated from the gorge by a wall and within the plantation is an area that looks very much like a charcoal-burning space. Even a cursory observer will note that the hill-top area was at one time coppiced, despite the fact that the last occasion was in 1940.

If you enter the wood from Combe Lane the first area worthy of attention is the village quarry, worked out now, but the origin of much of the building stone in the settlement. It, too, used to be delineated by a wall. Opposite the quarry to the north is Pigsfoot Wood, a remnant of the ancient Wild Wood, with small-leaved lime (Pry) and yellow archangel both present as indicators. Fifty years ago in spring this was carpeted with bluebells, now largely replaced by white-flowering ramsons.

Follow the path down to the bottom of the gorge and you find yourself surrounded by birdsong, snowberry and box shrubs. The path winds south, damp and shady, where golden saxifrage and small yellow balsam bloom. The latter was introduced in the late nineteenth century when the wood, as part of the estate, boasted arboreal promenades, or *bois orné*, very much a status symbol at that time.

The east side of the gorge is steep with a number of small unstable screes topped by crags some 150ft above. On the top of these crags is a section of calcareous grassland known to locals as 'the plateau'. Once upon a time it was close cropped by rabbits and covered an area half as much again; myxamatosis, shooting and vandalism, however, have hindered nature's management and permitted encroachment by scrub.

Some forty years ago grizzled skipper could be found laying their eggs on wild strawberry and cinquefoil plants which grew there but, alas, no longer. Another casualty is autumn fellwort, but happily ploughman's spikenard still occurs.

If you get the chance on an early summer morning, sit quietly on the edge of the northern plateau. All around is birdsong, the hum of insects and a seductive perfumery of woodland scents. Below, you look down upon the top of the gorge tree canopy and, if you are really lucky, a woodpecker or jay may fly across from one tree to another. It can be a simply magical experience.

The gorge is notable for its yew trees, one of which is at least a thousand years old. Where there is enough light *Rhododendron ponticum* flourishes: planted as game cover for Victorian shooting parties, it is an alien plant in England and a curse, killing most potential plant competitors. The rest of the woodland boasts a host of different tree species, both native and introduced, as well as a varied shrub layer, especially on the combe crags.

Above the gorge, if you search carefully, early-purple orchids and morels can be found. Blackcap sing by the plateau, great-spotted woodpecker drum to establish their territory, and a quiet interlude sitting under the trees will reveal fox, roe deer and, at dusk, badger. To the east of the wood two ponds are used by great-crested newt for breeding. For most of the year these amphibians live in the wood's leaf-litter and hibernate in crevices among rocks. The ponds are 'dew ponds' purposely created to provide livestock with a source of water: constructed from puddled clay, they are held in place and protected by stone walls and a flagstone floor.

Running across the middle of the wood in an arc are eighteenth-century boundary stones marked 'S' and 'G' – on the north side was the Sparrow estate and, to the south, the Gore holding. These stones are rare and listed; they date from well before the various branches of the Gibbs gained possession of the Tyntesfield and Barrow estates.

Sadly, at the time of writing, yet more evidence of disrespect for the natural environment abounds. Whether as a result of vandalism, mountain bikes or scattered litter, parts of the woodland are being systematically desecrated by human activity, aided and abetted in a more subtle way by an unchecked grey squirrel population – another alien to British shores.

Scree on the east side of the combe gorge. These piles of stones are formed by frost cracking up the crags some 150ft above. Owing to milder winters over the last decade, rock fracturing has decreased allowing much of the scree to stabilize.

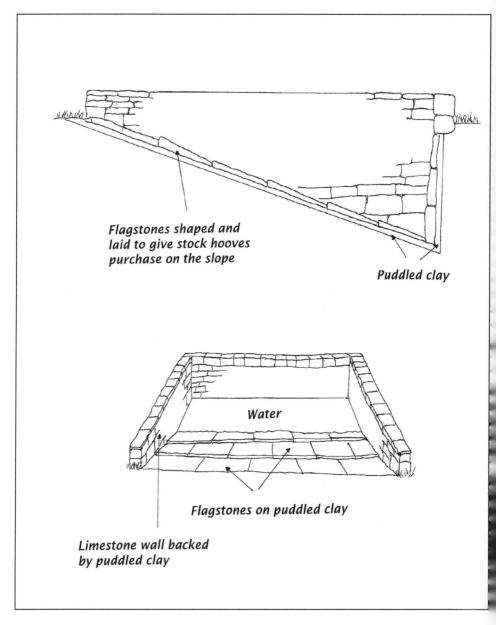

Flagstones shaped and
laid to give stock hooves
purchase on the slope

Puddled clay

Water

Flagstones on puddled clay

Limestone wall backed
by puddled clay

Plan and cross-section showing the construction of a North Somerset dew pond.

12

❦

Jewels in the Crown: St Michael's Church

T HE other equally resplendent jewel in the village's crown is the Church of St Michael and All Angels. Up until the twentieth century, when piecemeal development spread eastward, the church was located at the very heart of the settlement. Only recently has it been discovered how significant a heritage site it is.

Until now all guides, histories and references to St Michael's have dated the early structure to AD 1140, during the reign of the fourth Norman king, Stephen; more precisely, to the middle of the civil war between the king and his cousin, Matilda. It is difficult to see why a settlement of probably no more than four families (and serfs at that) would warrant the construction of a stone church. However, fresh evidence strongly suggests that the church could have been constructed some hundred years earlier when a thane was in residence and the settlement enjoyed the associated prestige. Such a situation would more readily call for an appropriately fashioned place of worship.

The main stumbling-block to this hypothesis has been the outer façade of the south doorway. It certainly looks like late Norman, as indeed it probably is, put there to emphasize

Norman ownership. Early manorial deeds for Wraxall indicate that Bourton was part of the manor, held from the Conquest by the Bishop of Coutances, who also at that time owned the manor of Backwell. As we have already mentioned, though, close inspection of the façade reveals that it is simply 'stuck on' to the doorway. Moreover, all published references, so far, observe how narrow and high the south doorway is while inside it is plain and undecorated: a feature of Saxon churches was that they were narrow and high. An examination by regional archaeologist, Mr Vince Russett (recommended by the noted Professor Mick Aston), identified the inner south doorway, chancel arch, font, lower half of the chancel and south nave walls as late Saxon work. He also confirmed the Saxon origin of the St Michael sculpture and the long and short quoins of the chancel. Further confirmation was provided by repointing work carried out in the autumn of 2006, which showed the stones of the lower walls to be set on each other 'dry'.

We therefore have good reason to believe that St Michael's was constructed somewhat earlier than has until recently been supposed. Mr Russett suggested a date range of 1040–80 but, if subsequent assumptions are correct (cf. Chapter 2), the range may well be narrowed to 1040–66. The reason for St Michael's retaining so much original fabric could be owing to the downgrading of the settlement after the Conquest of 1066: the church became a mere chapelry of Wraxall which was the main Norman manor of the area.

For most of its existence Bourton has been a very small community, lacking endowment since 1066, which appears to have conserved the building except for two phases. After the Black Death of 1348 many churches in England were neglected and fell into a state of disrepair, not least because the common roofing material of the time (thatch) required regular renewal, being prone to natural decay. The 2006 repointing work to the church also revealed what happened sometime between 1350 and 1450 – the period of architectural style known as 'perpendicular'. During these years the Saxon windows, which were rather small, were replaced by the present frames, the west wall was knocked down and replaced by the great arch and tower that you see today, and the south porch was added. Probably the now filled-up doorway in the chancel wall was also inserted. A new roof was constructed and the coved ceiling installed, with the spaces between the ribs filled with laths and plaster.

There was clearly an active priest at this time because church building maintenance was a joint responsibility of community and priest. The mass dial on the porch gives further credence to this. Structurally, there is little else known or identified until the early part of the nineteenth century, except for the effect of a violent storm at some point in the eighteenth century when a pinnacle of the tower was blown down and, instead of being replaced, was cut up and used as the base of the pulpit.

The tower housed three bells, one of which is dated 1718. Sometime around 1770 two of the bells fell to the ground and shattered – apparently, their wooden supporting framework had decayed. It is not known if all three bells had been made at the same time or if the surviving bell was a replacement for an earlier one. What we do know is that the fragments were sold for £28 in 1826 in order to finance the construction of an 8ft x 8ft vestry on the north side of the chancel. This may have been a reaction to what happened in the previous year, when a warrant had been issued against a certain Mark Lott for 'stealing part of a broken bell out of the belfry'.

There are only two bells in the tower now, which are more than adequate; three bells could hardly be called a peal. Besides the 1718 casting there is a little 'ting-tang' which might be the relocated Sanctus bell that used to be outside, above the chancel arch. Inside, a groove in the arch stonework, rubbed by the bell-pull rope, can be detected.

Up to the Reformation some parts of the interior were brightly painted: traces of red ochre can still be identified on the chancel arch and on the base of the font.

In general terms, life in a small rural community consisted of manual work, largely to provide food, clothing and shelter, all revolving around the seasons of the year and the functions of the Church. There was very limited time for leisure activity, so church festivals and devotions provided a welcome break. This pattern continued for centuries certainly from the end of Roman occupation until, in some settlements, the outbreak of the First World War.

Church records for Bourton do not exist prior to 1701, and then there are only registers of births, marriages and deaths. Not until 1802 do snippets begin to appear that help to build up a picture of events during the nineteenth century, although we continue to be vexed or baffled by a paucity of information in many instances. For example, in 1803 a note reads: 'Churchyard wall built', but which one? There are four! Then in 1825 another states: 'The churchyard wall from west to south built'. Bearing in mind the church is located east to west, where was the west to south wall? On the other hand, in 1833 'the Chancel and Nave slated' is perfectly clear.

It is edifying to glean from the parish books that, for the first half of the nineteenth century, the 'Sacrament of the Lord's Supper' was administered only four times a year: Christmas, Easter, Whitsun and Michaelmas. From 1850 to 1880 it was celebrated once each month, and after 1880 fortnightly and on all Holy Days. This contrasts sharply with present practice where almost every service includes it.

For most of the nineteenth century there was a gallery in the tower. Since the village population was around 200 the accommodation of a gallery for extra seating is not surprising. This was further aided in 1852 when 'eleven square pews' were 'replaced by twenty two narrow ones'. At the same time, the north wall of the nave was repaired and the outer surface of all walls repointed.

In 1881 our Victorian predecessors embarked upon fifteen years of drastic alterations. Beginning with the demolition of the north nave wall and construction of the north aisle, the works were completed in 1895 with an extension beside the chancel. This meant that the vestry of 1826 had to be demolished, being in the way. The organ was then moved into the extension.

Three years before this final Victorian adaptation there was a fire in the church. A piece of wood had been left in the packing over the hot-air flue of the heating apparatus. The wood extended under parquet flooring, so when it ignited it set light to the floor, then spread to a seat and several stools. Fortunately, the sexton discovered the fire and managed to extinguish the flames successfully, thus averting a possible disaster. Overall, the damage amounted to £5 6s. 4d.

Sharp-eyed visitors, on first encountering the south aspect of the church, will notice the blocked-up doorway in the chancel wall. I have always wondered about its small dimensions and can only assume that villagers of the fifteenth century were, at the very least, slimmer than their twenty-first-century counterparts. Strangely enough, we do know a little about its history: it was blocked up in 1826 on an instruction from the Bishop and, at the same time a privy was removed from the north side of the churchyard. I seems that it was not unusual for a member of the congregation to slip out during a service to take advantage of this handy facility. Services and sermons could be lengthy in the seventeenth century!

The churchyard itself is noteworthy. According to Revd Collinson, the yew tree was mature in 1791. Since then it has received a very necessary source of nourishment from the interred corpses, but it is far from being large. A recorded minute of 24 October 1812 reads:

The Churchyard was consecrated for burials.

It is claimed that, up to then, the dead were buried in any adjoining parish that would accept them, but we have no idea what happened in mediaeval times; it is most likely that some burials were beside the church because the population was so small. Between 1812 and 1889 at least 250 bodies were interred in that very confined space. In 1889 the churchyard was closed; the corpses must have been stacked up on one another. Fortunately, Mr Anthony Gibbs of Tyntesfield, who by then was patron of the church, donated a piece of land on the other side of the road as a cemetery. That too is now closed and contains over 200 burials.

In the south-east corner of the churchyard is the base and socket of a preaching cross believed to be a late fourteenth-century installation. It is a listed structure, as are the 'chest' tombs. Much of the stone used for grave-marking is of poor quality and a good many stones have lost their inscriptions; the location adjacent to the now heavily polluted A370 does not help durability. In the chest tomb to the west of the tower lie the bodies of John Lewis, Yeoman, and his wife, Hester. John, who died after his wife in 1858, held the land and properties to the west of the church.

In 1959, for purely ecclesiastical purposes, 600 acres of Long Ashton were annexed to Flax Bourton Rectory bringing Cambridge Batch, Clevedon Road properties and Gatcombe into the pastoral care of the Priest-in-Charge; but they remain to this day in the civil administration of Long Ashton.

The Church of St Michael and All Angels, replete with its traditions and festivities, has clearly played a major role in the life and development of our village. The church building itself not only serves as a fascinating testament to Flax Bourton's heritage and history, but stands in its own right as a simple, unpretentious structure – a veritable Saxon gem without equal in Northern Somerset and Bristol.

One of several unusual features to be found in the churchyard: a remnant of a late fourteenth-century preaching cross. The shaped stone on top was the 'cap' of a Sanctus bell housing located above the chancel arch roof.

The pulpit surmounts the redeployed tower pinnacle, beside the magnificent chancel arch.

St Michael's nave and chancel after a period of extensive Victorian rebuilding. Note the oil lamp lighting installation and choir pews in the chancel.

Epilogue

※

Flax Bourton in the Third Millennium

THE story of our village has presented us with a mixed bag of insights and intrigues, superstitions and speculations, personalities and power struggles. But always at its heart has been its very own time capsule, St Michael's Church. From this, we have deduced that the Norman Conquest forced Bourton into the feudal system and yet, because of its location, it still retained its own identity. We know too, from our time capsule, that despite outbreaks of the Black Death some of the village population survived to put the community back on its feet, and late mediaeval records of gifts indicate that the 'Chapel of Burton' was held in regard. We can see around us remnants of the village's development during the seventeenth and eighteenth centuries, and what impact there was from the coming of nineteenth-century technology.

But throughout our exploration, one unifying theme has more or less held the rest together: Flax Bourton, during its many years of existence, has been intimately connected with the land. Its rich agricultural resources, and the way it has exploited them, have enabled the village to flourish as an independent, self-contained community right up until the twentieth century.

Now that the link with the environment has been largely lost, severed as it seemed to be in little more than a decade, can it be rediscovered in the twenty-first century? Unless there is a completely fresh impetus given to our current economic and social climate, it does seem unlikely. The European Union's detached control, a lack of vision from successive governments, supermarket culture monopolizing and supplying every need, the loss of traditional skills in the workplace, and a relentlessly competitive infrastructure: all these factors contribute towards the demise of modest rural communities such as our own.

But there can be hope. If we ourselves are prepared to become that fresh impetus and, as local residents, have the desire to acknowledge and value our heritage, then we can take determined measures to ensure that it survives to be cared for and carried on by our children. Flax Bourton has a flourishing school, a lively church, a village pub, a new community centre and a growing population, all surrounded by an outstanding landscape. True, most of us are undoubtedly influenced by urban lifestyles these days for better or worse; many are also dependent upon the rich economic and cultural opportunities afforded by nearby Bristol itself. In a bid to re-establish a harmonious relationship with the environment, I am not suggesting that our village be preserved in aspic; it never has been a rural retreat disconnected from contemporary life. Rather, being uniquely placed to present a cohesive bridge between rural and urban communities, perhaps it is up to us to take the initiative in embracing possible ways forward in the wider quest for a sustainable future. Perhaps villages like our own can lead the way 'back to the land'.

As a start, it would be wonderful if, for example, the whole village could together acquire and conserve Bourton Combe and its wood. In its own right it is a heritage site of special archaeological, historical, botanical and geological interest; link all that to the village itself and its importance is huge. So come on, fellow villagers: let us resolve to make the opening chapter of the third millennium really memorable.

A view of the village across the valley from Bourton Combe.

Appendix 1

❦

Properties Originally of Listed Status

Bourton House	II	The Cottage (St Michael's House)	III
Hereford House	III	Castle Farm	III
The Laurels	II	Church Farm	II
Angel Inn/Old Angel		Priory Farm	II
Cottage	II	Old Rectory	II
Old Post Office	III	St Michael's Church	II*

Appendix 2

❦

1838 Tithe Redemption Map

Only four properties are named on the reproduction overleaf; the following key may therefore help to locate others:

2	Porch Cottage	39	Rock Cottage
4	The Laurels	42	Grange Farm
7	Grove Cottage	48	Primrose Cottage
16	Church Farm		(that was)
18	The Castle	78/79	Castle Farm
27	The Cottage	88	The 'Old Grange'
	(St Michael's House)	152	Flax Lea (currently)
30	Priory Farm	158	Wayside Cottage

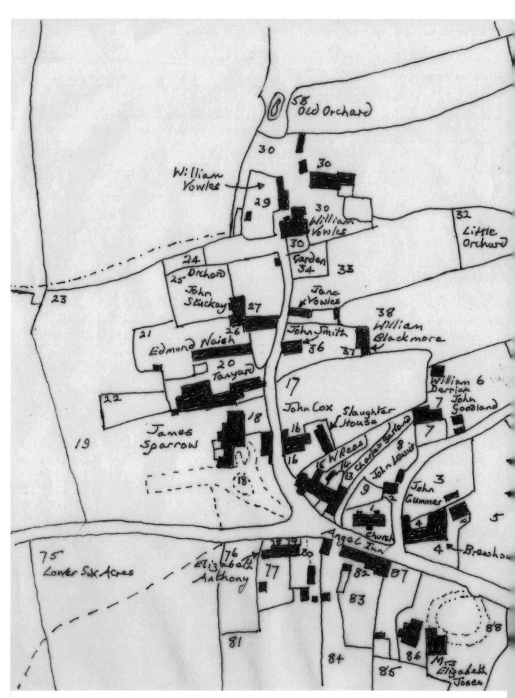

A redrawing based upon the Tithe Redemption Map of 1838. Notice how most of the dwellings and church keep to the higher ground above the 'marsh'. The field names are indicative of wet ground and many of the south–north field boundaries had or were rhynes. Also note the existence of five orchards at this period.

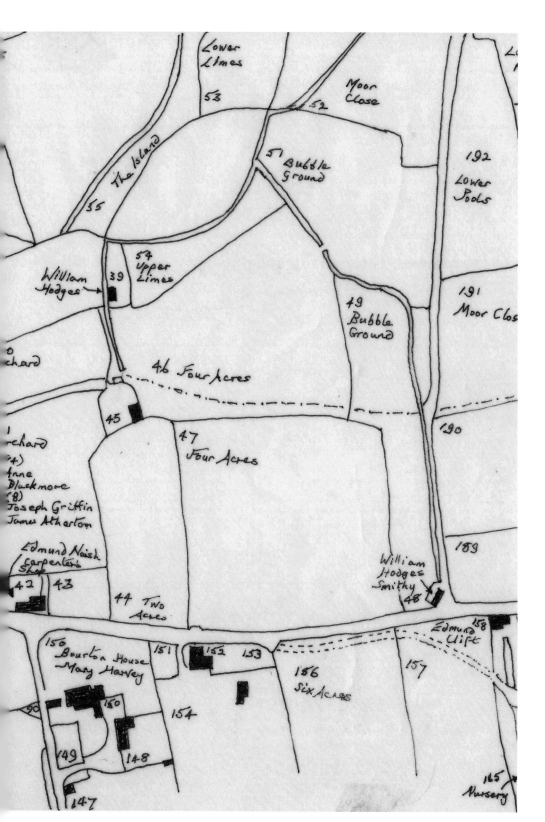

Further Reading

꙳

Collinson, J. *The History and Antiquities of the County of Somerset* (3 volumes) (1791)

Gardner, K.S. *Who Made the Land Yeo? Study in the Landscape Archaeology of Somerset's North Marsh (Pennant Special)* (1998)

Glasse, G.H. *The Maid of the Haystack* (1801)

Greenhill, B.J. *The Parish Church of St Michael and All Angels, Flax Bourton* (1960)

Hill, R. *One Hundred Years in the Village School of Flax Bourton* (1959)

Master, G.S. *A Parochial History of Flax Bourton* (1893)

Morris, J. (Ed.) *History from the Sources: Domesday Book, Somerset* (1980)

Quinn, P. *Holy Wells of the Bath and Bristol Region* (1999)

Somerset Record Office and Archives:
http://www.somerset.gov.uk/archives

Tiller, K. *English Local History: An Introduction* (1992)

Wright, B. *Somerset Dragons* (2002)

Index

✿

References in italic text denote illustrations.